Key Stage 3
Years 7–9
Science
10-Minute Tests

Track progress with 10-minute skills checks

Published in the UK by Scholastic, 2023

Scholastic Education, Bosworth Avenue, Warwick, CV34 6UQ

SCHOLASTIC and associated logos are trademarks and/or registered trademarks of Scholastic Inc.

© Scholastic, 2023

2 3 4 5 6 7 8 9   4 5 6 7 8 9 0 1 2 3

A CIP catalogue record for this book is available from the British Library.

ISBN 978-0702-32684-4

Printed and bound by Bell & Bain, Glasgow, UK.

The book is made of materials from well-managed, FSC®-certified forests and other controlled sources.

Due to the nature of the web we cannot guarantee the content or links of any site mentioned.

We strongly recommend that teachers check websites before using them in the classroom.

Every effort has been made to trace copyright holders for the works reproduced in this book, and the Publishers apologise for any inadvertent omissions.

www.scholastic.co.uk

For safety or quality concerns:
UK: www.scholastic.co.uk/productinformation
EU: www.scholastic.ie/productinformation

Author
Danny Nicholson

Editorial team
Rachel Morgan, Vicki Yates, Aidan Gill, Eric Pradel and Michelle Oldfield

Design
Dipa Mistry and Andrea Lewis

Illustration
David Rojas Marquez, scientific illustrator & PhD

Technical drawings
QBS Learning

Contents

How to use this book

This book contains 24 science tests. Each test should take about 10 minutes to complete. The tests are divided into biology, physics and chemistry, with six tests at the end covering a mixture of these different subjects.

The tests are designed to help make sure you understand the essential concepts and skills involved, and to identify where you need to revise and study more.

Many questions have a short answer line to write on. But some may ask you, amongst other things, to tick something, fill in a table or draw on a diagram. Read the question carefully. For some questions you may need extra paper for your workings.

The total number of marks per test can be found at the end of each test. The marks for each question are given on the right-hand side.

Answers can be found at the end of the book on pages 58–63. On page 64 is a progress tracker where you can record your mark and note any area you may need to go back and review.

1. Here is a diagram of an animal cell.

   a. Name each labelled part of the cell.

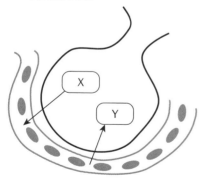

A: _____

B: _____

C: _____

D: _____

(4 marks)

   b. If this was a plant cell, give **two** other parts you would expect to see.

    i. _____   ii. _____

(2 marks)

2. Gas exchange takes place inside our lungs. Our lungs contain millions of air sacs called alveoli.

   a. Give **three** ways that alveoli are well adapted for gas exchange to occur.

    i. _____

    ii. _____

    iii. _____

(3 marks)

b. What is the type of blood vessel that is shown in the diagram?

_____ *(1 mark)*

c. Arrows X and Y show the exchange of gases between the blood and alveoli.

i. What gas passes in direction X?   _____ *(1 mark)*

ii. What gas passes in direction Y?   _____ *(1 mark)*

iii. Name the process by which the gases move through the walls of the alveoli during gas exchange.

_____ *(1 mark)*

3. The digestive system processes food after it has been eaten.

a. Explain why we need to digest our food.

_____

(1 mark)

b. Give the name of the type of chemical that speeds up the digestion of food.

_____ *(1 mark)*

c. Give **two** functions of hydrochloric acid in the stomach.

i. _____

ii. _____

(2 marks)

The finger-like structures inside the small intestine are called villi.

d. How do villi make sure the digested food is absorbed quickly?

_____

(1 mark)

Total	/18

1. Here is a diagram of the male reproductive system.

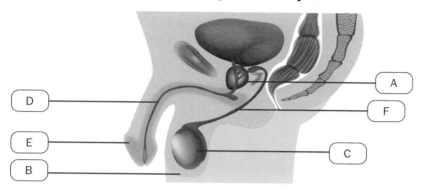

a. Which letter labels the sperm duct? _____ *(1 mark)*

b. Which letter labels a testis? _____ *(1 mark)*

c. Which letter labels the part where sperm cells are made? _____ *(1 mark)*

2. All living things carry out a process called respiration.
   Respiration is the process by which living organisms release energy from glucose.

a. Name the part of the cell where respiration takes place.

_____ *(1 mark)*

b. Oxygen is usually required for respiration to take place. Name this type of respiration.

_____ *(1 mark)*

c. Write a word equation for this type of respiration.

_____ *(2 marks)*

d. Name the type of respiration which takes place without oxygen.

_____ *(1 mark)*

e. Write a word equation for this type of respiration in humans.

_____ *(2 marks)*

3. The menstrual cycle involves preparing the uterus to receive a fertilised egg.

    a. On day 1, the lining of the uterus begins to break down. What is this process called?

    _____

                               (1 mark)

    b. On day 14, an egg is released. Which part of the female reproductive system produces the egg?

    _____

                               (1 mark)

    c. Name the process in which an egg is released.

    _____

                               (1 mark)

    d. The lining of the uterus gets thicker between day 14 and day 28. Why does the lining build up during this time?

    _____

                               (1 mark)

4. A balanced diet consists of the correct proportions of different nutrients. Explain why we need the following nutrients in our diet.

    a. carbohydrates

    _____

                               (1 mark)

    b. proteins

    _____

                               (1 mark)

    c. fats

    _____

                               (1 mark)

    d. fibre

    _____

                               (1 mark)

Total	/18

1. The human skeleton has several different roles: to protect, support and allow movement.

   a. Which part of the skeleton protects:

   i. the brain? _____

   (1 mark)

   ii. the lungs? _____

   (1 mark)

   b. Many bones have bone marrow inside them. What does bone marrow produce?

   _____

   (1 mark)

2. The nucleus inside cells contains a chemical called DNA.

   a. What does DNA stand for?

   _____

   (1 mark)

   b. A coiled-up length of DNA is called a chromosome. How many chromosomes are there in a normal, human body cell?

   _____

   (1 mark)

   c. How many chromosomes are there in a human sperm cell?

   _____

   (1 mark)

   d. Explain the difference between the numbers of chromosomes in parts b and c.

   _____

   _____

   (2 marks)

3. The diagram shows the muscles and bones in the arm.

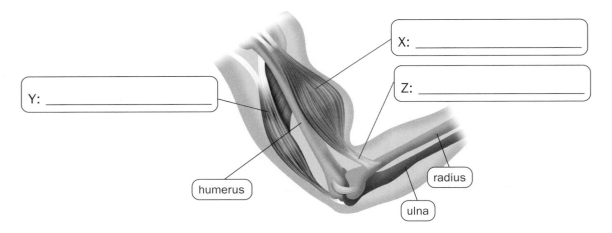

X: _____

Z: _____

Y: _____

humerus

radius

ulna

a. Name muscles X and Y.   *(2 marks)*

b. Z is a tissue that connects muscles to bones. What do we call Z?   *(1 mark)*

c. Muscles X and Y are a pair of antagonistic muscles. Explain why some
muscles work as an antagonistic pair.

_____

(1 mark)

d. Describe what happens to the lower arm when each of the following occurs.

i. Muscle X contracts.

_____

(1 mark)

ii. Muscle Y contracts.

_____

(1 mark)

4. This diagram shows a simple food chain from a garden.

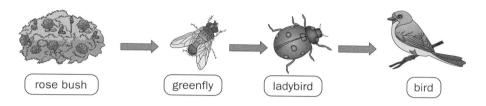

rose bush → greenfly → ladybird → bird

  a. Which of these organisms is a producer?

_____

(1 mark)

  b. Which of these organisms are consumers?

_____

(1 mark)

  c. If the gardener sprayed the rose bushes with a chemical to kill the greenfly, which organism would probably be the worst affected by this?

_____

(1 mark)

  d. Explain your answer to part c.

_____

_____

(2 marks)

  e. What word do we use to describe how the organisms in an environment depend on each other to survive?

_____

(1 mark)

Total	/20

Biology Test 4

1. Here is a diagram of a knee joint.

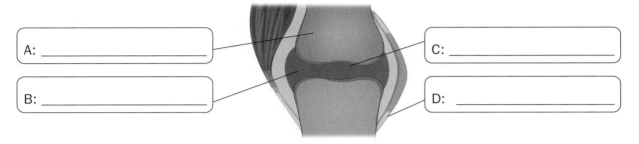

A: _____

B: _____

C: _____

D: _____

    a. Label the parts of the joint A–D. *(4 marks)*

    b. Which two parts of a joint prevent the bones from rubbing together?

        i. _____

        ii. _____ *(2 marks)*

    c. Give an example of each of these joints in the body.

        i. ball and socket joint _____ *(1 mark)*

        ii. hinge joint _____ *(1 mark)*

        iii. pivot joint _____ *(1 mark)*

2. It is possible to calculate the force a muscle applies to a bone. Look at this example:

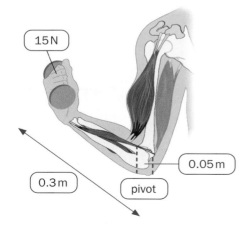

15 N

0.3 m

0.05 m

pivot

a. Calculate the moment of the weight. Use the equation below.

moment of a force = force × distance of force from pivot

Moment = _____ N m

(1 mark)

b. Use the moment to calculate the force applied by the muscle. Show your working.

Force = _____

(2 marks)

3. a. Classify the following drugs as legal or illegal, by writing them in the appropriate box.

aspirin   LSD   caffeine   alcohol   cocaine   tobacco

Legal	Illegal

(6 marks)

b. What is the general name for a type of drug which makes someone see or hear things that are not there?

_____

(1 mark)

c. What effect does a depressant have on the body?

_____

(1 mark)

d. What effect does a stimulant have on the body?

_____

(1 mark)

e. Some drugs have side effects. Explain what is meant by "side effect".

_____

(1 mark)

Total	/22

13

Biology Test 5

1. The diagram shows a section through a flower.

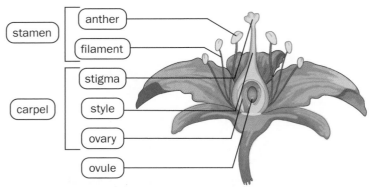

a. Which part of the flower produces pollen?

_____

(1 mark)

b. On which part of the flower does the pollen land?

_____

(1 mark)

c. Complete these sentences.

When a pollen grain arrives on the flower a _____ grows out of the

pollen grain. This grows down the _____ towards the ovary. The male pollen

and the female_____ join together. This is called _____.

(4 marks)

d. Which part of the flower becomes the seed?

_____

(1 mark)

2. The graph shows how height varies in a human population.

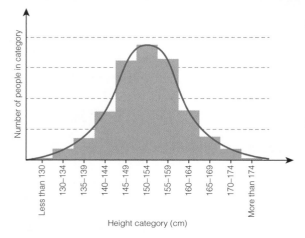

a. What type of variation does this graph show?

_____

(1 mark)

b. Give **two other** examples of a characteristic that shows this type of variation.

i. _____

ii. _____

(2 marks)

c. What do we call the type of variation shown by a characteristic such as eye colour?

_____

(1 mark)

3. The Amur leopard is classified as an endangered species.

a. What is meant by "endangered"?

_____

(1 mark)

b. Identify **two** possible changes in the environment that could lead to a species like the Amur leopard becoming endangered, and explain the effect of each change.

_____

_____

(2 marks)

c. We can try to protect animals such as the Amur leopard through conservation and gene banks.

i. Explain how conservation could protect the leopards.

_____

(1 mark)

ii. Which types of cell are stored in a gene bank?

_____

(1 mark)

iii. Explain how a gene bank could prevent the leopard from becoming extinct.

_____

(2 marks)

Total	/18

Biology Test 6

1. **The image shows the veins in a leaf.**

   a. Describe the function of the veins.

   _____

   (1 mark)

   b. On the underside of the leaves are tiny holes called stomata.
   What is the function of these holes?

   _____

   (1 mark)

   c. Why does the leaf have a waxy layer on the surface?

   _____

   (1 mark)

2. **Plants make their own food through photosynthesis.**

   a. Write down the word equation for photosynthesis.

   _____

   (2 marks)

   b. What green pigment is needed for photosynthesis to take place?

   _____

   (1 mark)

   c. In which cell components does photosynthesis take place?

   _____

   (1 mark)

   d. Give **two** ways that photosynthesis is important to humans.

   i. _____

   ii. _____

   (2 marks)

3. This is Alysha. The diagram shows some of her features.

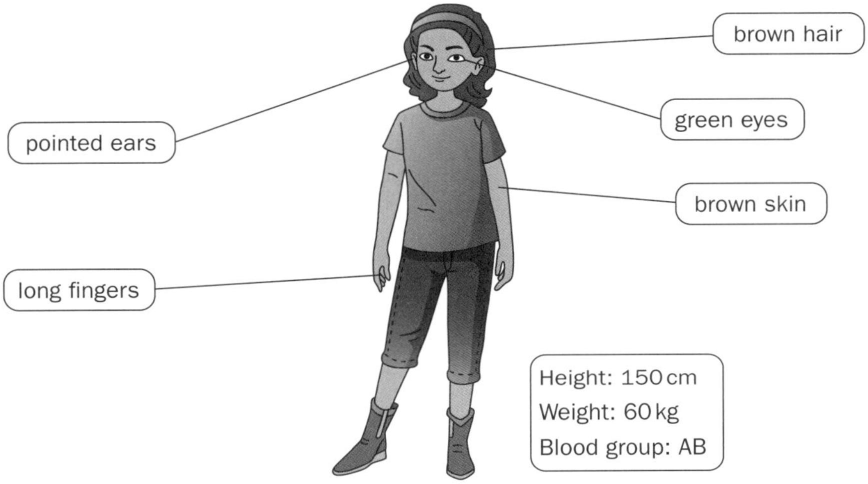

brown hair

green eyes

pointed ears

brown skin

long fingers

Height: 150 cm
Weight: 60 kg
Blood group: AB

Some of Alysha's features have been inherited from her parents.
Some of her features have also been affected by her environment.

Classify each feature in the table by writing its name and placing a tick
in the correct column.

Feature	Can **only** be inherited from her parents	Can **also** be affected by her environment
	☐	☐
	☐	☐
	☐	☐
	☐	☐
	☐	☐
	☐	☐
	☐	☐
	☐	☐

(8 marks)

Total   /17

Chemistry Test 1

1. The diagrams show the arrangement of particles in three different materials.

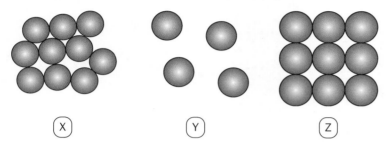

a. Which diagram shows a solid? _____ *(1 mark)*

b. Which diagram shows a liquid? _____ *(1 mark)*

c. Which diagram shows a gas? _____ *(1 mark)*

2. Here is a diagram of the changes of state from solid to liquid to gas.

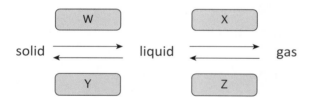

a. What changes of state are shown by boxes W, X, Y and Z?

W: _____ *(1 mark)*

X: _____ *(1 mark)*

Y: _____ *(1 mark)*

Z: _____ *(1 mark)*

b. Which **two** changes of state can take place when a material is heated?

(2 marks)

c. Which **two** changes of state can take place when a material is cooled?

(2 marks)

d. Some solids, such as dry ice, sublime when heated. What is meant by sublimation?

_____

(1 mark)

3. Here are the formulae for six different substances.

H_2	
H_2O	
O_2	

Ag	
Cu	
CO_2	

a. Write the names of the substances in the boxes. *(6 marks)*

b. Which of these substances are elements?

_____

(1 mark)

c. Which of these substances are compounds?

_____

(1 mark)

d. Which of these substances exist as single atoms?

_____

(1 mark)

e. Which of these substances exist as two or more atoms joined together?

_____

(1 mark)

Total	/22

Chemistry Test 2

1. **The table contains some characteristics of different materials.**

   Tick the ones that are appropriate for each type of material.
   Some may apply to more than one type of material.

Characteristic	Solid	Liquid	Gas
fixed shape	☐	☐	☐
changes shape to match container	☐	☐	☐
fixed volume	☐	☐	☐
fills whole container	☐	☐	☐
cannot be poured	☐	☐	☐
can be poured	☐	☐	☐
easily squashed	☐	☐	☐
hard to squash	☐	☐	☐

   (8 marks)

2. **A cooling curve for compound X is shown below.**

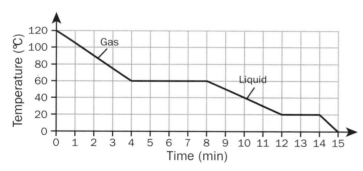

   a. What is the melting point of the compound? _____ °C   *(1 mark)*

   b. For how long was compound X cooling before it became completely solid?

   _____   *(1 mark)*

   c. Explain what was happening when the curve was flat.
   Refer to the particles of compound X in your answer.

   _____

   (2 marks)

3. The diagram below shows how to get pure water from sea water.

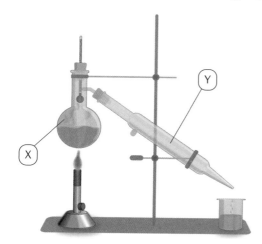

a. Name this process.

_____

(1 mark)

b. Describe what is happening at the location labelled X.

_____

(1 mark)

c. What temperature will the thermometer be showing while this is happening?

_____ °C

(1 mark)

d. Describe the process that takes place at the location labelled Y.

_____

(1 mark)

e. The water in the beaker is pure. What does **pure** mean?

_____

(1 mark)

4. **The flow chart shows how to get pure salt from rock salt, which is a mixture of salt and sand.**

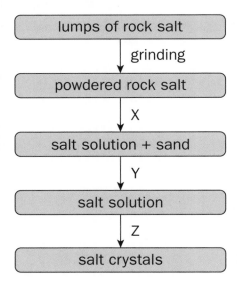

a. Name the process in step X.

_____

b. Describe how to do step Y. Include what apparatus you would use, and what happens to the salt and the sand.

_____

_____

(2 marks)

c. Name step Z.

_____

(1 mark)

Total	/21

1. Here is an outline of the periodic table.

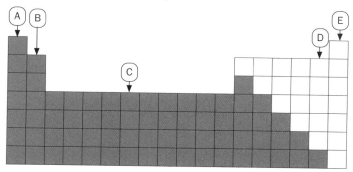

a. What name is given to the columns of the table?

_____

(1 mark)

b. What name is given to the rows of the table?

_____

(1 mark)

c. Which label (A–E) is above a column of soft, shiny metals that react vigorously with water?

_____

(1 mark)

d. Which area contains non-metals, the shaded area or the unshaded?

_____

(1 mark)

e. Look at the elements in column A. What happens to their reactivity as you go **down** the column?

_____

(1 mark)

f. Look at the elements in column D. What happens to their reactivity as you go **down** the column?

_____

(1 mark)

g. What can you say about the reactivity of the elements in column E?

_____

(1 mark)

2. The pH scale ranges from 0 to 14.

a. What is the pH of a neutral solution?

_____

(1 mark)

b. What is the pH of a strongly acidic solution?

_____

(1 mark)

c. Solution X has a pH of 14. How would you describe solution X?

_____

(1 mark)

d. What is an indicator?

_____

(1 mark)

e. Complete the table below to show the colour of the indicator at each pH value.

Indicator	Colour at pH 1	Colour at pH 14
universal indicator		
litmus paper		

(4 marks)

3. Complete these word equations for the different reactions of acids with metal compounds.

a. acid + metal → _____ *(1 mark)*

b. acid + metal oxide → _____ *(1 mark)*

c. acid + metal hydroxide → _____ *(1 mark)*

d. acid + metal carbonate → _____ *(1 mark)*

Total	/19

1. A piece of magnesium ribbon is burned in air.

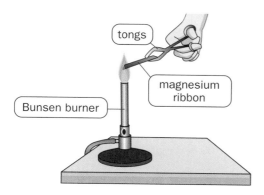

a. The magnesium reacts with the oxygen in the air to produce a white powder. What is the name of the substance that is produced?

_____

(1 mark)

b. Write a word equation for this reaction.

_____

(2 marks)

c. When magnesium burns, energy is released as heat and light. Is this reaction endothermic or exothermic?

_____

(1 mark)

d. Why must you use tongs to hold the ribbon, instead of your fingers?

_____

(1 mark)

e. Why should you not look directly at the magnesium as it burns?

_____

(1 mark)

2. The diagram shows copper carbonate being heated in a test tube.

a. What are the products of this chemical reaction?

_____

(1 mark)

b. Write a word equation for this reaction.

_____

(2 marks)

c. What is the name given to this type of chemical reaction?

_____

(1 mark)

d. What colour is the copper carbonate powder at the start of the reaction?

_____

(1 mark)

e. What colour is the powder at the end of the reaction?

_____

(1 mark)

3. Ismail mixes hydrochloric acid with sodium hydroxide solution in a beaker.

a. What type of reaction will take place?

_____

(1 mark)

b. What are the products of this reaction?

_____

(2 marks)

c. Write a word equation for this reaction.

_____

(2 marks)

d. If Ismail mixes the correct amounts of acid and alkali, the solution should have a pH of 7.

   i. What can he use to make sure he adds just the right amount of acid?

   _____

(1 mark)

   ii. How would Ismail know when the pH is 7?

   _____

(1 mark)

e. What can Ismail do to get salt crystals from the solution?

_____

(1 mark)

Total	/20

Chemistry Test 5

1. a. Put the following metals in order from the least reactive to the most reactive:

potassium   zinc   silver   aluminium   platinum   calcium   iron

Least reactive _____

_____ Most reactive

(3 marks)

b. Carbon is not a metal, but it can be put in the reactivity series.
Where would you put carbon in the sequence you wrote for part a?

_____

_____

(2 marks)

2. Decide whether or not a reaction would occur in each of the following situations. For each situation, explain your reasoning.

a. Zinc metal is added to copper sulfate solution.

Will a reaction occur? _____

Reason: _____

(2 marks)

b. Iron metal is added to magnesium sulfate solution.

Will a reaction occur? _____

Reason: _____

(2 marks)

c. Calcium metal is added to iron sulfate solution.

Will a reaction occur? _____

Reason: _____

(2 marks)

3. When molten rock is underground, we call it magma.

a. What do we call magma if it comes to the surface?

_____

(1 mark)

b. Basalt is an example of a rock formed from magma when it cools.

What type of rock is basalt? _____ *(1 mark)*

c. If a rock of this type has large crystals, does this suggest that the rock cooled

underground or on the surface? _____ *(1 mark)*

d. Explain your answer to part c.

_____

(1 mark)

4. The diagram shows part of the carbon cycle.

a. Name process W. _____

(1 mark)

b. Name process X. _____

(1 mark)

The amount of carbon dioxide in our atmosphere is
increasing, mostly due to human activity.

c. Give **two** ways that humans have affected the levels of carbon dioxide in the last 100 years.

i. _____

ii. _____ *(2 marks)*

d. Carbon dioxide is a greenhouse gas. Explain how greenhouse gases are
affecting the average temperature of the Earth's atmosphere.

_____

(1 mark)

e. Why are fossil fuels known as non-renewable fuels?

_____

(1 mark)

Total	/21

Chemistry Test 6

1. **Three metals are placed into test tubes of water.**

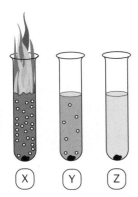

X   Y   Z

Identify which metal, X, Y or Z, could be:

a. gold _____   *(1 mark)*

b. potassium _____   *(1 mark)*

c. calcium _____   *(1 mark)*

2. **Iron is a useful metal, commonly found in the ground as its ore, iron oxide. To extract the iron, we can heat it with carbon and limestone in a very hot furnace.**

a. Why is the carbon able to displace the iron in iron oxide?

_____   *(1 mark)*

b. What gas is produced?

_____   *(1 mark)*

c. Why is limestone used in the furnace?

_____

_____   *(1 mark)*

d. Identify the substance that runs out of the bottom of the furnace.

_____   *(1 mark)*

e. What do we call a chemical reaction where oxygen is removed from a compound?

_____   *(1 mark)*

f. Balance this equation for the reaction that takes place in the furnace:

$\boxed{}$ $C(s)$ + $\boxed{}$ $Fe_2O_3(s)$ → $\boxed{}$ $CO_2(g)$ + $\boxed{}$ $Fe(l)$ *(2 marks)*

3. a. Label this diagram of the Earth to name the different layers.

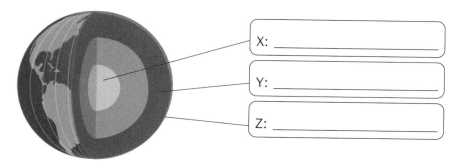

X: _____

Y: _____

Z: _____

(3 marks)

b. Which layer of the Earth is mainly made from iron and nickel?

_____

(1 mark)

c. Which layer of the Earth is made from semi-solid molten rock?

_____

(1 mark)

d. What is the most common element found in part Z?

_____

(1 mark)

4. The Earth's atmosphere is made up of many different gases. The pie chart shows the three main gases.

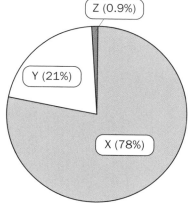

a. What are the names of the gases shown?

X: _____

Y: _____

Z: _____

(3 marks)

b. Name another gas present in the atmosphere.

_____

(1 mark)

| Total | /20 |

Physics Test 1

1. You cannot see a force, but you can see the effect it has on an object. Complete the sentences below to describe the effects of forces.

    a. A force can make a stationary object start to _____.   *(1 mark)*

    b. If an object is moving, a force is needed to make it _____,

    _____ or _____.   *(3 marks)*

    c. A sideways force can make a moving object change its _____.   *(1 mark)*

    d. A squashing force can make an object change its _____.   *(1 mark)*

2. Two jumbo jets are flying on the same path. Plane A is travelling at 900 km/h. Plane B is behind it, travelling at 820 km/h.

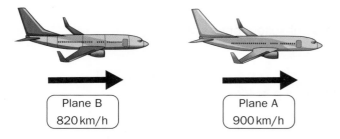

| Plane B |
| 820 km/h |

| Plane A |
| 900 km/h |

    a. What is the speed of plane A relative to plane B?

    Relative speed = _____ km/h   *(2 marks)*

    b. The planes are currently 10 km apart. After 2 hours, how far apart will they be?

    Distance apart: _____ km   *(2 marks)*

3. The diagram shows a car driving along a road.

   a. Name the force produced by the car's engine.

   _____

(1 mark)

   b. As well as friction between the tyres and the road surface, what other force pushes backwards on the car as it moves forwards?

   _____

(1 mark)

   c. Use the size of the force arrows in the diagrams below to describe what is happening to each car. Circle the correct answer.

    i.

The car is **speeding up / slowing down / moving at a steady speed**.   *(1 mark)*

    ii.

The car is **speeding up / slowing down / moving at a steady speed**.   *(1 mark)*

    iii.

The car is **speeding up / slowing down / moving at a steady speed**.   *(1 mark)*

Total	/15

Physics Test 2

1. There are two types of force: contact and non-contact.

For each force in the table below, place a tick to show whether it is a contact or a non-contact force.

Type of force	Contact	Non-contact
magnetic	☐	☐
friction	☐	☐
gravity	☐	☐
static electricity	☐	☐
upthrust	☐	☐
air resistance	☐	☐

(6 marks)

2. Amelia is investigating how to balance weights on a metre ruler. The ruler is pivoted in the middle. She has set up the weights like this.

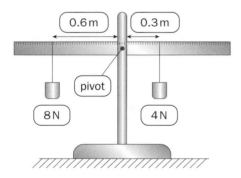

a. Calculate the anticlockwise moment to the left of the pivot.

Anticlockwise moment = _____ Nm

(2 marks)

b. Calculate the clockwise moment to the right of the pivot.

Clockwise moment = _____ Nm

(2 marks)

c. What will happen to the metre ruler? Circle the correct answer.

remain stationary / rotate anticlockwise / rotate clockwise

(1 mark)

3. **Four cars took part in a classic car rally but none of the cars finished the race. The table shows some of the race information.**

Team	Distance travelled (km)	How long car stayed in race (hours)	Average speed (km/h)
Alpha	130	2	
Bravo	180		60
Charlie	100	2	
Delta		2.5	56

a. Write the equation for calculating speed.

_____

(1 mark)

b. Calculate and complete the information missing from the table.   *(4 marks)*

c. Which team drove the fastest? _____   *(1 mark)*

Team Echo also took part in the race. Here is a distance-time graph for their car.

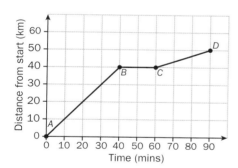

d. For how long was their car stationary?

_____ minutes   *(1 mark)*

e. Between which two points were they travelling the fastest?

From point _____ to point _____.

(1 mark)

f. Team Echo had to abandon their race after 90 minutes. How far had they travelled in this time?

Distance = _____ km

(1 mark)

Total	/20

35

Physics Test 3

1. A boat is floating on a river. The diagram shows the forces acting on it.

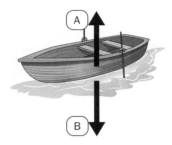

   a. Complete the sentences.

   i. The downwards force, B, is equal to the boat's _____.   *(1 mark)*

   ii. The upwards force, A, acting on the boat is called _____.   *(1 mark)*

   b. The boat is floating. What does that tell you about the size of force A compared to force B?

   _____ *(1 mark)*

2. Cassie used the apparatus shown to investigate the extension of a spring when adding different masses. The spring remains below its elastic limit at all times. Her recordings are shown in the table.

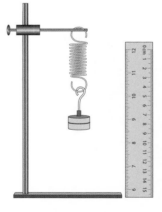

Mass (N)	Reading (cm)	Extension (cm)
0	10	0
20	25	15
40	40	
60	55	
80	70	

   a. Complete the table with the values for the extension of the spring.   *(3 marks)*

   b. Complete this sentence.

   Hooke's law says that the extension of the spring is directly _____ to the force applied to it.   *(1 mark)*

   c. Use the data to predict the expected extension for a mass of 30 N.

   _____ cm   *(1 mark)*

3. The Earth is one of eight planets that orbit the Sun.

a. Which planet is nearest to the Sun? _____ *(1 mark)*

b. Which is the largest planet orbiting the Sun? _____ *(1 mark)*

c. Pluto is no longer classed as a planet. What type of celestial object is Pluto?

_____ *(1 mark)*

d. Explain why Neptune has the longest year of the eight planets.

_____

(1 mark)

e. Explain why planets orbit the Sun.

_____

(1 mark)

4. The diagrams here show different circuits using identical bulbs. The battery has a potential difference of 12 V.

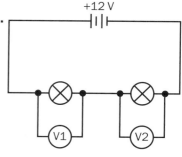

a. What is the potential difference measured at V1 and V2?

V1 = _____ V

V2 = _____ V

(2 marks)

b. The components are rearranged into a parallel circuit. What is the potential difference measured at V1 and V2 now?

V1 = _____ V

V2 = _____ V

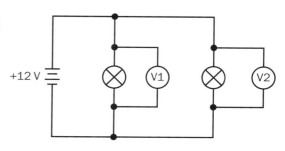

(2 marks)

Total	/17

Physics Test 4

1. The diagram shows the two forces acting on a parachutist after her parachute has opened.

a. What force acts downwards on the parachutist (force A)?

_____ *(1 mark)*

b. What force is acting upwards on the parachutist (force B)?

_____ *(1 mark)*

c. The two forces are the same size. What can you say about the speed of the parachutist? Circle **one** answer.

Her speed is **increasing** / **is decreasing** / **stays the same**. *(1 mark)*

2. The diagram below shows Earth. The arrow shows the direction of light from the Sun.

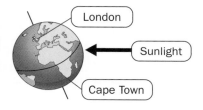

a. Which city is currently experiencing summer – London or Cape Town?

_____ *(1 mark)*

b. Explain why the tilt of the Earth gives us seasons.

_____

_____

(2 marks)

c. What do we call the day of the year with the least number of daylight hours?

_____ *(1 mark)*

d. What do we call the days in spring/autumn when day and night are the same length?

_____ *(1 mark)*

e. Briefly explain why we add a leap day into the calendar, and how often this occurs.

_____

_____

(2 marks)

3. The gravitational field strength at the surface of planet Earth is about 10 N/kg.

a. Write the equation for calculating the weight of an object on Earth.

_____

(1 mark)

b. Calculate the weight on Earth of a person with a mass of 60 kg.

_____ N

(1 mark)

The same person travels to Mars, where the gravitational field strength is 3.7 N/kg.

c. Calculate their weight on Mars.

_____ N

(1 mark)

d. What **two** factors affect the strength of the gravitational attraction between two objects?

i. _____   ii. _____

(2 marks)

4. A student set up this circuit with an unknown resistor.

a. Complete these sentences.

A conductor is a material with a _____ resistance.

An insulator is a material with a _____ resistance.

(2 marks)

b. The ammeter measured 3 A. The voltmeter measured 12 V. Calculate the resistance of the resistor R. (Remember that resistance = voltage ÷ current.)

_____ Ω

(1 mark)

c. The resistor R was replaced with a 2 Ω resistor. The voltmeter still read 12 V. What would be the reading on the ammeter?

_____ A

(2 marks)

Total	/20

Physics Test 5

1. Two magnets were placed close together as shown in the diagram.

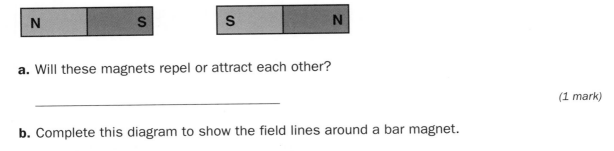

   a. Will these magnets repel or attract each other?

   _____   *(1 mark)*

   b. Complete this diagram to show the field lines around a bar magnet.

   (2 marks)

2. Energy can be stored in different ways.

   Draw lines to connect each object with the energy store that it has.

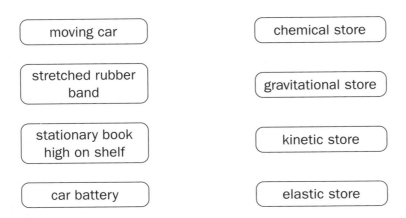

   (4 marks)

40

3. This question is about work done by forces.

   a. State the equation for calculating work done.

   _____

   (1 mark)

   b. Calculate the energy transferred (work done) in each of these situations.

   i. A box weighing 40 N is lifted to a shelf 2 m high.

   _____ J

   (2 marks)

   ii. A toy boat is blown by the wind with a force of 6 N across a 10 m pond.

   _____ J

   (2 marks)

   iii. A person weighing 700 N climbs up a 3 m ladder.

   _____ J

   (2 marks)

4. The diagram shows some different features of a wave.

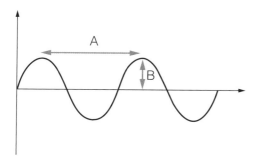

   a. What do we call distance A? _____ *(1 mark)*

   b. What do we call distance B? _____ *(1 mark)*

   c. What type of wave is a water wave? Circle the correct answer.

   transverse / longitudinal *(1 mark)*

   d. Give another example of this type of wave.

   _____ *(1 mark)*

| Total | /18 |

Physics Test 6

1. Toby wound a coil of wire around a nail and attached it to a battery.

   a. What do we call this type of magnet?

   _____ *(1 mark)*

   b. Circle the materials that would be attracted to the magnet.

      pencil eraser   glass marble   steel paper clip   iron nail   plastic pen   *(1 mark)*

   c. Give two ways that Toby could make the magnet stronger.

      i. _____

      ii. _____

      (2 marks)

2. Energy cannot be made or destroyed; it is just moved from one energy store to another. Complete the sentences for these energy transfers.

   a. Dropping a brick: Energy is transferred from its _____ store to

      its _____ store. *(1 mark)*

   b. Releasing a catapult: Energy is transferred from its _____ store to its

      _____ store. *(1 mark)*

   c. Burning coal: Energy is transferred from its _____ store to a _____

      store. Some energy is also transferred as _____ energy. *(2 marks)*

3. A student shines a laser at a mirror at an angle of 60°, as shown in the diagram.

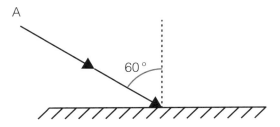

a. Draw the path of the reflected light ray on the diagram. *(1 mark)*

b. What is the name of the dotted line on the diagram, perpendicular to the mirror?

_____ *(1 mark)*

c. How is the angle of reflection related to the angle of incidence?

_____

(1 mark)

d. Light reflecting off a mirror in this way is an example of what type of reflection?
Circle the answer.

specular / diffuse *(1 mark)*

4. A ray of light shines into a glass block. Three possible paths for the light ray are A, B and C.

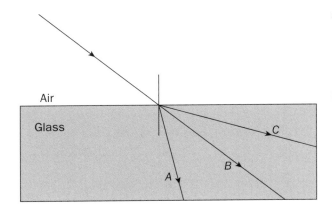

a. Which arrow shows the correct path the light would take inside the glass block?

_____ *(1 mark)*

b. Name the process that changes the direction of light in this way.

_____ *(1 mark)*

43

5. An oscilloscope is connected to a microphone.
   The diagram shows the pattern observed on the oscilloscope screen.

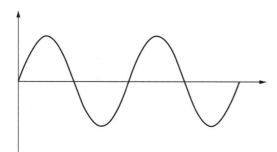

Complete these sentences.

a. The frequency is the number of waves per _____.   *(1 mark)*

b. The higher the frequency, the _____ the pitch of the sound.   *(1 mark)*

c. Frequency is measured in _____.   *(1 mark)*

d. Increasing the amplitude will increase the _____ of the sound.   *(1 mark)*

Total		/18

1. Draw lines to match the parts of the digestive system with their roles.

A. mouth

B. stomach

C. liver

D. small intestine

E. large intestine

1. Contains hydrochloric acid. Breaks down proteins.

2. Makes bile to break fat into droplets.

3. Products of digestion and water are absorbed here.

4. Breaks down food into chunks. Produces saliva.

5. Food which cannot be broken down passes through here.

(5 marks)

2. 10 g of salt is added to 50 g water and stirred until it dissolves.

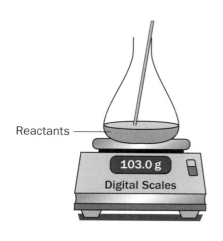

Reactants

103.0 g

Digital Scales

a. What is the total mass of the salt solution?

Total mass = _____ g

(1 mark)

b. What substance is the solvent?

_____

(1 mark)

c. What substance is the solute?

_____

(1 mark)

d. If all the water is evaporated, what mass of salt will be left behind?

_____

(1 mark)

3. A pinhole camera is a very simple camera without a lens. Light passes through a hole in the front and an image forms on the screen at the back.

    a. Draw light rays from the top and bottom of the tree to show how the image forms on the screen at the back of the camera. *(2 marks)*

    b. Is the image on the screen upside down or the correct way up?

    _____ *(1 mark)*

4. Louie weighs 600 N. The area of one of his feet is 0.01 m².
What is the total pressure below his feet in the following situations?

    a. Standing on one foot?

    Total pressure = _____ N/m² *(2 marks)*

    b. Standing on both feet?

    Total pressure = _____ N/m² *(1 mark)*

Louie puts on some skis. One ski has dimensions of 1.50 m × 0.08 m.

    c. What is the total pressure below the skis when he is wearing both of them? (Ignore the weight of the skis.)

    Total pressure = _____ N/m² *(2 marks)*

Total	/17

1. The diagram shows four different layers of sedimentary rock on a cliff.

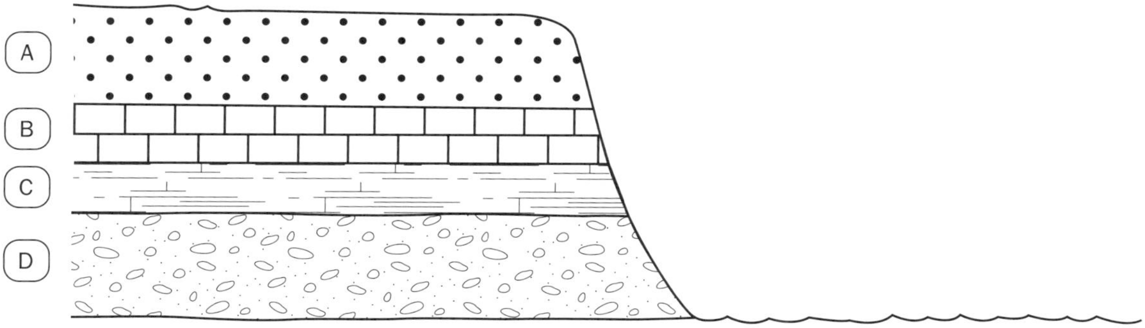

a. Which rock layer is the oldest? _____ (1 mark)

b. Which rock layer is the youngest? _____ (1 mark)

c. Using your knowledge of how sedimentary rocks form, explain why one layer of sedimentary rock can be older than another.

_____

_____

_____

(3 marks)

d. Layer C contains a fossil of an animal known to have lived between 60 and 80 million years ago. What is the oldest age this rock layer can be?

_____ (1 mark)

e. Explain why no fossils are ever found in igneous rock.

_____

(1 mark)

2. Scientists think that polar bears evolved from an isolated group of grizzly bears around 125 000 years ago. Within this population of bears, some of them had sharper teeth that were better for eating seals, which was the main food available in the frozen Arctic.

a. Complete the sentence:

When a population of organisms all have slightly different features, we call this

_____.   *(1 mark)*

b. Explain why more polar bears would be born with sharper teeth.

_____

_____

(3 marks)

c. Complete the sentence:

The process in which living things adapt and change over time is known as evolution through

_____ .   *(1 mark)*

d. Give **two** other ways that polar bears have adapted to survive in very cold climates.

i. _____

ii. _____   *(2 marks)*

3. Isabelle is studying the movement of smoke particles under a microscope.

a. Explain why the smoke particles appear to move randomly.

_____

_____

(2 marks)

b. What is the name for this type of movement shown by the particles of smoke?

_____   *(1 mark)*

4. A loaf of bread is removed from a hot oven and left on a rack to cool down.

Roan puts her hand close to the loaf of bread without touching it. She can feel the heat from the bread on her hand.

a. How is heat being transferred to her hand without touching the bread?

_____

(1 mark)

The bread is left on the rack for a while.
Thermal energy is transferred from the bread to the air around it.

b. What happens to the temperature of the bread?

_____

(1 mark)

c. What happens to the temperature of the air?

_____

(1 mark)

d. Complete the sentence:

When the bread and the air are the same temperature, we say they have reached

_____ .

(1 mark)

Total	/21

Mixed Science Test 3

1. Match the fruit to the method of seed dispersal it is suitable for.
   Draw lines to show the connections.

sycamore seed

animal dispersal

tomato

wind

water

conker

drop and roll

coconut

(4 marks)

2. Complete these sentences about metals reacting with air.

a. When iron is heated to a high temperature, it reacts with _____
from the air.   *(1 mark)*

b. When a metal reacts with oxygen it forms _____.   *(1 mark)*

c. When you burn iron filings in a Bunsen flame in air, the iron joins with oxygen

to form _____.   *(1 mark)*

d. When burned, copper reacts with air to form _____.

The brown-coloured copper changes colour to _____.   *(2 marks)*

3. A balloonist drops a sandbag over the edge of their balloon and it falls to the ground.

a. At what point does the sandbag have the most gravitational potential energy?

_____

(1 mark)

b. At what point does it have the most kinetic energy?

_____

(1 mark)

4. Label this diagram of the eye.

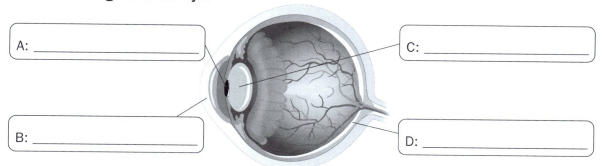

A: _____

C: _____

B: _____

D: _____

(4 marks)

5. The diagram shows a speedboat on a lake.

a. Label the forces A, B and C.

A _____

B _____

C _____

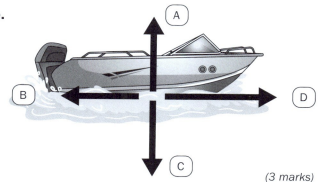

(3 marks)

b. If the boat is floating, what does that tell you about the size of force A compared to force C?

_____

(1 mark)

c. The boat is travelling forwards at an increasing speed.
What does that tell you about the size of force D compared to force B?

_____

(1 mark)

d. What is the benefit of giving the boat a streamlined shape?

_____

(1 mark)

Total	/21

Mixed Science Test 4

1. **Name the following chemical compounds.**

   a. MgO _____   *(1 mark)*

   b. CO_2 _____   *(1 mark)*

   c. $CuSO_4$ _____   *(1 mark)*

   d. Fe_2O_3 _____   *(1 mark)*

   e. $CaCO_3$ _____   *(1 mark)*

2. **During gestation, the fetus develops in the womb. It is connected to the mother through the placenta.**

   a. What **two** things does the fetus get from the mother through the placenta?

   i. _____

   ii. _____   *(2 marks)*

   b. What **two** things does the fetus pass to the mother via the placenta?

   i. _____

   ii._____   *(2 marks)*

   c. Explain why a baby can be harmed if the mother smokes or takes drugs during pregnancy.

   _____

   (1 mark)

3. **When a metal spoon is placed into a hot drink, the end of the spoon furthest from the drink will eventually feel hot. Complete the sentences to explain what happens:**

Heating one end of a metal spoon makes the particles inside

it _____ more.

They gain energy in their _____ energy stores.

Energy is transferred along the rod by particles _____ into their neighbouring particles.

Energy is transferred from the _____ end to the _____ end.

This process is known as _____.

(6 marks)

4. **The diagram shows how the atoms are arranged in different substances.**

a. Which box contains a pure element? _____ *(1 mark)*

b. Which box contains a single compound? _____ *(1 mark)*

c. Which box contains a mixture of two compounds? Explain your answer.

_____

_____

(2 marks)

Total	/20

Mixed Science Test 5

1. **All living things are made from cells. Complex living things, such as humans, are made from trillions of cells, organised into tissues, organs and organ systems.**

   a. Describe the difference between a tissue and an organ.

   _____

   (1 mark)

   b. What is an organ system?

   _____

   (1 mark)

   c. Briefly describe the function of each of these organ systems.

   i. circulatory system

   _____

   (1 mark)

   ii. respiratory system

   _____

   (1 mark)

   iii. nervous system

   _____

   (1 mark)

   iv. digestive system

   _____

   (1 mark)

2. **What are the roles of these parts of the eye in helping us to see?**

   a. lens _____ *(1 mark)*

   b. cornea_____ *(1 mark)*

   c. iris_____ *(1 mark)*

   d. retina_____ *(1 mark)*

3. The fire triangle shows the three things needed for a fire to take place.

a. What are the three sides of the fire triangle?

i. _____

ii. _____

iii. _____

(3 marks)

b. Name the chemical reaction that takes place when something burns.

_____

(1 mark)

c. A firefighter might spray a special foam onto a fire to put it out. Explain how the foam makes the fire go out.

_____

(1 mark)

4. A television set has a power rating of 100 W.

a. How many joules of energy does the television transfer every second?

_____

(1 mark)

b. How much energy would the television transfer in one hour? _____ J

(1 mark)

5. An electric oven has a power rating of 2 kW. The oven is left on full power for 3 hours.

a. How many kWh of energy did it use? _____ kWh

(1 mark)

b. If 1 kWh costs 16 pence, how much did it cost to run the oven? _____

(1 mark)

Total	/19

Mixed Science Test 6

1. Decide if each of the following properties best describes a metal or a non-metal and tick the correct box for each property.

	Metal	Non-metal
electrical insulator	☐	☐
shiny	☐	☐
malleable	☐	☐
low melting point	☐	☐
ductile	☐	☐

(5 marks)

2. The image shows a paper chromatogram for four different inks A to D. A mystery ink, X, was also tested to see which inks it contained.

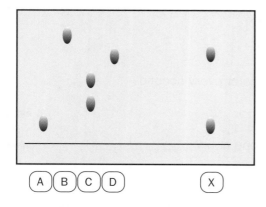

a. Which ink is the most soluble? _____ *(1 mark)*

b. Ink X is a mixture of which inks A to D? _____ *(1 mark)*

3. Light travels incredibly fast. The speed of light is approximately 300,000 km/s.

a. Calculate how far light can travel in one minute.

_____ km *(2 marks)*

b. Light from the Sun takes about 8 minutes to reach us.
Calculate how far away the Sun is from Earth.

_____ km

(2 marks)

c. What is a light-year?

_____

(1 mark)

d. The star Alpha Centauri is 4.3 light-years away from Earth.
How long does it take light from Alpha Centauri to reach the Earth?

_____

(1 mark)

e. Use your knowledge of sound and light waves to explain how we
can see the Sun, but not hear it.

_____

(1 mark)

**4. Wind-pollinated and insect-pollinated flowers look very different. In the table, put a tick
against the features you would expect to find in each type of flower.**

Feature	Insect-pollinated	Wind-pollinated
Bright petals	☐	☐
Strong, pleasant smell	☐	☐
Dull petals	☐	☐
No scent	☐	☐
Small, light pollen grains	☐	☐
Feathery stigmas	☐	☐
Larger, sticky pollen grains	☐	☐

(7 marks)

Total	/21

Answers

Q	Biology Test 1 (pages 5–6)	Marks
1	**a.** A: nucleus, B: cell membrane, C: cytoplasm, D: mitochondria (1 mark each)	4
	b. Any two from: cell wall, chloroplasts, vacuole (1 mark each)	2
2	**a.** Any three from: thin, good blood supply, large surface area (1 mark each)	3
	b. capillary	1
	c. i. oxygen / O_2	1
	ii. carbon dioxide / CO_2	1
	iii. diffusion	1
3	**a.** large substances need to be broken down/made smaller so can be absorbed	1
	b. enzyme	1
	c. i. kills harmful bacteria	1
	ii. lowers pH so enzymes can work	1
	d. give a large surface area (for absorption)	1
	Total	**18**

Q	Biology Test 2 (pages 7–8)	Marks
1	**a.** F	1
	b. C	1
	c. C	1
2	**a.** mitochondria	1
	b. aerobic	1
	c. glucose + oxygen ➔ carbon dioxide + water (1 mark for reactants, 1 mark for products)	2
	d. anaerobic	1
	e. glucose ➔ lactic acid (1 mark for reactants, 1 mark for products)	2
3	**a.** menstruation/period	1
	b. ovary	1
	c. ovulation	1
	d. preparing to receive the (fertilised) egg	1
4	**a.** provide energy	1
	b. growth	1
	c. used for energy (allow insulation)	1
	d. helps food move through intestines	1
	Total	**18**

Q	Biology Test 3 (pages 9–11)	Marks
1	**a. i.** skull	1
	ii. ribs or ribcage	1
	b. blood cells	1
2	**a.** deoxyribose nucleic acid	1
	b. 46 (allow 23 pairs)	1
	c. 23	1
	d. In sexual reproduction, two cells (sperm and ovum/ egg) fuse/join, so number of chromosomes in each cell is half that of body cell. (1 MARK????)	2
3	**a.** X: biceps, Y: triceps (1 mark each)	2
	b. tendon	1
	c. Muscles cannot push, so one contracts/pulls while the other relaxes.	1
	d. i. arm goes up	1
	ii. arm goes down	1
4	**a.** rose bush	1
	b. greenfly, ladybird, bird	1
	c. bird	1
	d. the chemical would accumulate up the food chain	2
	e. interdependent/interdependence	1
	Total	**20**

Q	Biology Test 4 (pages 12–13)	Marks
1	**a.** A: bone (femur), B: (lubricating) fluid, C: cartilage, D: ligament (1 mark each)	4
	b. cartilage, fluid (1 mark each)	2
	c. i. shoulder/hip	1
	ii. knee/knuckle/toe	1
	iii. neck	1
2	**a.** moment = 15 × 0.3 = 4.5 Nm	1
	b. force = moment ÷ distance = 4.5 ÷ 0.05 = 90 N (1 mark for correct working but wrong answer)	2
3	**a.** (1 mark per correct answer)	6

Legal		Illegal	
aspirin	caffeine	LSD	cocaine
alcohol	tobacco		

Q	Biology Test 4 (pages 12–13)	Marks
	b. hallucinogen	1
	c. slows down the nervous system	1
	d. speeds up the nervous system/makes someone more alert	1
	e. unwanted/unpleasant effect of a drug	1
	Total	**22**

Q	Biology Test 5 (page 14–15)	Marks
1	a. anther *or* stamen	1
	b. stigma	1
	c. When a pollen grain arrives on the flower a **pollen tube** grows out of the pollen grain. This grows down the **style** towards the ovary. The male pollen and the female **egg** (or **ovule**) join together. This is called **fertilisation**. (1 mark per correct word)	4
	d. the egg/ovule	1
2	a. continuous	1
	b. Any two of: weight, foot length, hand span, arm span, (or any other valid answer) (1 mark each)	2
	c. discontinuous	1
3	a. not many are left/at risk of going extinct	1
	b. Any two from: forests being cut down so loss of habitat/homes, hunted/poached meaning more are killed, climate change leading to loss of habitat or food source (1 mark each)	2
	c. i. (provides) safe areas for leopards to live	1
	ii. sperm and eggs	1
	iii. for breeding / if numbers get too low (1 mark each)	2
	Total	**18**

Q	Biology Test 6 (pages 16–17)	Marks
1	a. carry water to the leaf (allow take glucose away)	1
	b. allow gases in/out of leaf (*or* allow oxygen out and carbon dioxide in)	1
	c. prevents/reduces water loss	1
2	a. carbon dioxide + water ➔ glucose + oxygen (1 mark for reactants, 1 mark for products)	2
	b. chlorophyll	1
	c. chloroplasts	1
	d. i. produces the food/sugar we eat	1
	ii. produces oxygen that we breathe	1
3	(table below)	8 (1 mark each)

Feature	Can **only** be inherited from her parents	Can **also** be affected by her environment
green eyes/ eye colour	✓	
brown hair/ hair colour		✓
brown skin/ skin colour		✓
pointed ears	✓	
height		✓
weight		✓
blood group (AB)	✓	
long fingers	✓	

	Total	**17**

Q	Chemistry Test 1 (pages 18–19)	Marks
1	a. Z	1
	b. X	1
	c. Y	1
2	a. W: melting, X: evaporating/boiling, Y: freezing/ solidfying, Z: condensing (1 mark each)	4
	b. W, X (allow melting, evaporating/boiling) (1 mark each)	2
	c. Y, Z (allow freezing/solidfying, condensing) (1 mark each)	2
	d. Changes straight from solid to gas (no liquid stage).	1
3	a. (1 mark each)	6

H_2	hydrogen		Ag	silver
H_2O	water		Cu	copper
O_2	oxygen		CO_2	carbon dioxide

Q		Marks
	b. hydrogen, oxygen, silver, copper *or* H_2, O_2, Ag, Cu (1 mark for all)	1
	c. water, carbon dioxide *or* H_2O, CO_2 (1 mark for all)	1
	d. silver, copper *or* Ag, Cu (1 mark for all)	1
	e. hydrogen, water, oxygen, carbon dioxide *or* H_2, H_2O, O_2, CO_2 (1 mark for all)	1
	Total	**22**

Q	Chemistry Test 2 (pages 20–22)	Marks
1	(1 mark per correct answer) (table below)	8

Characteristic	Solid	Liquid	Gas
fixed shape	✓		
changes shape to match container		✓	✓
fixed volume	✓	✓	
fills whole container			✓
cannot be poured	✓		
can be poured		✓	✓
easily squashed			✓
hard to squash	✓	✓	

Q		Marks
2	a. 20 °C	1
	b. 8 minutes	1
	c. (1 mark for each of the below) compound X was solidifying/freezing/becoming a solid particles lose energy and join together	2
3	a. distillation	1
	b. water turning to steam/liquid to gas/boiling/ evaporating	1
	c. 100 °C	1
	d. condensing/condensation	1
	e. contains no other substances	1
4	a. dissolving	1
	b. Use a filter funnel/filter paper. Pour the salt solution plus sand through a funnel. Salt solution goes through, sand left on paper. (1 mark for two parts)	2
	c. evaporation	1
	Total	**21**

Answers

Q	Chemistry Test 3 (pages 23–24)	Marks
1	**a.** groups	1
	b. periods	1
	c. A	1
	d. unshaded	1
	e. reactivity increases	1
	f. reactivity decreases	1
	g. not reactive/unreactive	1
2	**a.** 7	1
	b. 1 (allow 1–3)	1
	c. strongly alkaline	1
	d. chemical that changes colour to show pH (*or* how acidic/alkaline)	1
	e. (1 mark each)	4

Indicator	Colour at pH 1	Colour at pH 14
universal indicator	red	purple
litmus paper	red	blue

Q	Chemistry Test 3 (pages 23–24)	Marks
3	**a.** salt (allow metal salt) + hydrogen	1
	b. salt (allow metal salt) + water	1
	c. salt (allow metal salt) + water	1
	d. salt (allow metal salt) + water + carbon dioxide	1
	Total	**19**

Q	Chemistry Test 4 (pages 25–27)	Marks
1	**a.** magnesium oxide	1
	b. magnesium + oxygen ➔ magnesium oxide (1 mark for reactants, 1 mark for products)	2
	c. exothermic	1
	d. gets very hot, will burn you	1
	e. very bright / will damage your eyes	1
2	**a.** copper oxide, carbon dioxide (both needed for 1 mark)	1
	b. copper carbonate ➔ copper oxide + carbon dioxide (1 mark for reactants, 1 mark for products)	2
	c. thermal decomposition	1
	d. green	1
	e. black	1
3	**a.** neutralisation	1
	b. sodium chloride, water (1 mark each)	2
	c. hydrochloric acid + sodium hydroxide -> sodium chloride + water (1 mark for reactants, 1 mark for products)	2
	d. i. indicator/universal indicator	1
	ii. will turn green	1
	e. evaporate the water	1
	Total	**20**

Q	Chemistry Test 5 (pages 28–29)	Marks
1	**a.** Least reactive: platinum, silver, iron, zinc, aluminium, calcium, potassium: Most reactive (half a mark per metal in the correct position, 3 marks maximum)	3
	b. below zinc,	1
	above aluminium	1
2	**a.** Reaction: yes	1
	Reason: zinc displaces/is more reactive than copper	1
	b. Reaction: no	1
	Reason: iron does not displace/is less reactive than magnesium	1
	c. Reaction: yes	1
	Reason: calcium displaces/is more reactive than iron	1
3	**a.** lava	1
	b. igneous	1
	c. underground	1
	d. cools slowly or crystals have time to grow	1
4	**a.** respiration	1
	b. photosynthesis	1
	c. burning fossil fuels, deforestation (1 mark each)	2
	d. traps heat from Sun, atmosphere is warming up	1
	e. they take millions of years to form, humans are using them faster than they are formed (allow not easily/ quickly replaced)	1
	Total	**21**

Q	Chemistry Test 6 (pages 30–31)	Marks
1	**a.** Z	1
	b. X	1
	c. Y	1
2	**a.** carbon is more reactive than iron (allow iron is less reactive than carbon)	1
	b. carbon dioxide	1
	c. to remove impurities	1
	d. (molten) iron	1
	e. reduction	1
	f. $3C(s) + 2Fe_2O3(s) ➔ 3CO_2(g) + 4Fe(l)$ (half a mark per number)	2
3	**a.** X: core, Y: mantel, Z: crust (1 mark each)	3
	b. core	1
	c. mantle	1
	d. oxygen	1
4	**a.** X: nitrogen, Y: oxygen, Z: argon (1 mark each)	3
	b. Any one from: carbon dioxide, water vapour (allow any other valid gas)	1
	Total	**20**

Q	Physics Test 1 (pages 32–33)	Marks
1	a. move b. speed up, slow down, stop, change direction (1 mark each for any 3) c. direction d. shape	1 3 1 1
2	a. relative speed = fastest speed – slowest speed *or* 900 – 820 = 80 km/h (2 marks for correct answer, 1 mark for correct working and wrong answer) b. (80 × 2) + 10 = 170 km (2 marks for correct answer, 1 mark for correct working and wrong answer)	2 2
3	a. thrust b. air resistance (allow drag) c. i. slowing down ii. moving at a steady speed iii. speeding up	1 1 1 1 1
	Total	15

Q	Physics Test 2 (pages 34–35)	Marks
1	(1 mark each)	6

Type of force	Contact	Non-contact
magnetic		✓
friction	✓	
gravity		✓
static electricity		✓
upthrust	✓	
air resistance	✓	

Q		Marks
2	a. moment = force × perpendicular distance *or* moment = 8 × 0.6 = 4.8 Nm (2 marks for correct answer, 1 mark for correct working and wrong answer) b. moment = force × perpendicular distance *or* moment = 4 × 0.3 = 1.2 Nm (2 marks for correct answer, 1 mark for correct working and wrong answer) c. rotate anticlockwise	2 2 1
3	a. (average) speed = distance ÷ time) b. (1 mark each)	1 4

Team	Distance travelled / km	How long car stayed in race / hours	Average speed / km/h
Alpha	130	2	**65**
Bravo	180	**3**	60
Charlie	100	2	**50**
Delta	**140**	2.5	56

Q		Marks
	c. Alpha d. 20 minutes e. From point **A** to point **B**. f. 50 km	1 1 1 1
	Total	20

Q	Physics Test 3 (pages 36–37)	Marks
1	a. i. weight ii. upthrust b. they are the same/equal	1 1 1
2	(1 mark each)	3

Weight / N	Reading / cm	Extension / cm
0	10	0
20	25	15
40	40	**30**
60	55	**45**
80	70	**60**

Q		Marks
	b. proportional c. 22.5 cm (allow 22 or 23)	1 1
3	a. Mercury b. Jupiter c. dwarf planet d. Neptune is the planet furthest from the Sun, so takes longest to complete an orbit e. force of gravity between Sun and each planet	1 1 1 1 1
4	a. V1 = 6 V, V2 = 6 V (1 mark each) b. V1 = 12 V, V2 = 12 V (1 mark each)	2 2
	Total	17

Q	Physics Test 4 (pages 38–39)	Marks
1	a. weight (allow gravity) b. air resistance (allow drag) c. stays the same	1 1 1
2	a. Cape Town b. tilted towards Sun in summer or away in winter heat/light from Sun is more direct/concentrated in summer (1 mark each) c. winter solstice d. equinox e. Earth goes round the Sun in 365 and ¼ days. We add up the quarter days and add an extra day onto the calendar every 4 years. (1 mark each)	1 2 1 1 2
3	a. weight (of object) = mass (of object) × gravitational field strength b. weight = 60 × 10 = 600 N c. weight = 60 × 3.7 = 222 N (allow 220 N) d. mass of objects, distance between them (1 mark each)	1 1 1 2
4	a. A conductor is a material with a **low** resistance. An insulator is a material with a **high** resistance. (1 mark each) b. R = 12 ÷ 3 = 4 Ω c. R = V ÷ I or 2 = 12 ÷ I I = 6 A	2 1 2
	Total	20

Physics Test 5 (pages 40–41)

Q	Physics Test 5 (pages 40–41)	Marks
1	**a.** repel **b.** (1 mark for correct lines. 1 mark for arrows pointing from N to S) 	1 2
2	(1 mark per pair) 	4
3	**a.** work done = force × distance moved (by force) **b. i.** energy transferred (work done) = 40 × 2 = 80 J **ii.** energy transferred (work done) = 6 × 10 = 60 J **iii.** energy transferred (work done) = 700 × 3 = 2100 J (for i, ii, iii: 2 marks for correct answer, 1 mark for correct working and wrong answer)	1 2 2 2
4	**a.** wavelength **b.** amplitude **c.** transverse **d.** light (allow any named regions of electromagnetic spectrum)	1 1 1 1
	Total	**18**

Physics Test 6 (pages 42–44)

Q	Physics Test 6 (pages 42–44)	Marks
1	**a.** electromagnet **b.** steel paperclip, iron nail (1 mark for both) **c.** use more coils, increase the current (allow add batteries) (1 mark each)	1 1 2
2	**a.** gravitational, kinetic **b.** elastic, kinetic **c.** chemical, thermal, light (1 mark for two correct)	1 1 2
3	**a.** light ray reflecting at 60° on other side of normal **b.** normal **c.** angle of incidence = angle of reflection (allow they are the same) **d.** specular	1 1 1 1
4	**a.** A **b.** refraction	1 1
5	**a.** second **b.** higher **c.** hertz (allow Hz) **d.** volume (allow loudness)	1 1 1 1
	Total	**18**

Mixed Science Test 1 (pages 45–46)

Q	Mixed Science Test 1 (pages 45–46)	Marks
1	(1 mark per pair) 	5
2	**a.** 60 g **b.** water **c.** salt **d.** 10 g	1 1 1 1
3	**a.** (1 mark per line) **b.** upside down	2 1
4	**a.** pressure = force ÷ area = 600 ÷ 0.01 = 60 000 N/m² **b.** area is doubled so pressure is halved = 30 000 N/m² **c.** pressure = force ÷ area = 600 ÷ (2 × 0.08) = 3750 N/m² (for a and c: 2 marks for correct answer, 1 mark for correct working and wrong answer)	2 1 2
	Total	**17**

Mixed Science Test 2 (pages 47–49)

Q	Mixed Science Test 2 (pages 47–49)	Marks
1	**a.** D **b.** A **c.** (1 mark per part below) small pieces of rock/sediment sink to bottom of sea/lake these pieces are squashed together by high pressure oldest rock will be at bottom/newer rock forms on top of older rock. **d.** 80 million years **e.** dead animal/plant would burn up	1 1 3 1 1
2	**a.** variation **b.** (1 mark per part below) helps them survive/eat seals so more chance of becoming adults and having offspring with sharper teeth. **c.** natural selection **d.** Any two from: small ears, thick fur, blubber, large feet, white fur, black skin (1 mark each)	1 3 1 2
3	**a.** particles of smoke hit by fast-moving particles of air **b.** Brownian motion	2 1
4	**a.** radiation **b.** decreases/goes down **c.** increases/goes up **d.** thermal equilibrium	1 1 1 1
	Total	**21**

Q	Mixed Science Test 3 (pages 50–51)	Marks
1	(1 mark per pair) sycamore seed — wind; tomato — animal dispersal; conker — drop and roll; coconut — water	4
2	**a.** oxygen **b.** (metal) oxide **c.** iron oxide **d.** copper oxide, black (1 mark each)	1 1 1 2
3	**a.** as it leaves the balloon (allow 'at the start') **b.** just before it hits the ground	1 1
4	A: pupil, B: cornea, C: lens, D: retina (1 mark each)	4
5	**a.** A: upthrust, B: water resistance, C: weight (1 mark each) **b.** they are the same/equal **c.** force D is larger than force B **d.** reduces water resistance/drag	3 1 1 1
	Total	**21**

Q	Mixed Science Test 4 (pages 52–53)	Marks
1	**a.** magnesium oxide **b.** carbon dioxide **c.** copper sulfate **d.** iron oxide **e.** calcium carbonate	1 1 1 1 1
2	**a.** oxygen, food (1 mark each) **b.** carbon dioxide, waste (1 mark each) **c.** Harmful substances from smoke can be passed to the baby through the placenta and umbilical cord.	2 2 1
3	(1 mark per answer) Heating one end of a metal spoon makes the particles inside it **vibrate** more. They gain energy in their **kinetic** energy stores. Energy is transferred along the rod by particles **bumping/colliding** into their neighbouring particles. Energy is transferred from the **hotter/warmer** end to the **colder/cooler** end. This process is known as **conduction**.	6
4	**a.** C **b.** A **c.** B; Particles are two different combinations of different atoms. (1 mark for B, 1 mark for explanation)	1 1 2
	Total	**20**

Q	Mixed Science Test 5 (pages 54–55)	Marks
1	**a.** Tissue is one type of cells. Organ is made from several different tissues. **b.** group of organs working together **c. i.** transport oxygen/carbon dioxide around body **ii.** get oxygen in/carbon dioxide out of body **iii.** control the body **iv.** break down and absorb food (half a mark each)	1 1 1 1 1 1
2	**a.** changes the shape to focus the light **b.** focuses the light **c.** controls the amount of light entering the eye **d.** photosensitive cells to detect light	1 1 1 1
3	**a.** fuel, heat, oxygen (1 mark each) **b.** combustion **c.** removes access to oxygen	3 1 1
4	**a.** 100 J **b.** (energy = 100 J × 60 min × 60 sec) = 360 000 J or 360 kJ	1 1
5	**a.** (energy = power × time = 2000 × 3) = 6 kWh **b.** (cost = energy × unit price = 6 × 16p) = £0.96 or 96p (allow for errors carried forward from part a)	1 1
	Total	**19**

Q	Mixed Science Test 6 (pages 56–57)	Marks
1	(1 mark each)	5

	Metal	Non-metal
electrical insulator		✓
shiny	✓	
malleable	✓	
low melting point		✓
ductile	✓	

Q		Marks
2	**a.** B **b.** A and D	1 1
3	**a.** distance = speed × time = 300 000 × 60 = 18 000 000 km **b.** distance = 18 000 000 × 8 = 144 000 000 km (for a, b: 2 marks for correct answer, 1 mark for correct working and wrong answer) **c.** distance light travels in one year **d.** 4.3 years **e.** Light waves can travel through the vacuum of space, sound waves cannot.	2 2 1 1 1
4	(1 mark each)	7

Feature	Insect-pollinated	Wind-pollinated
bright petals	✓	
strong, pleasant smell	✓	
dull petals		✓
no scent		✓
small, light pollen grains		✓
feathery stigmas		✓
larger, sticky pollen grains	✓	

| | **Total** | **21** |

Progress Tracker

Write down your mark for each question and the total for the test to track your progress.

Test	Mark	Area to review
Biology Test 1		
Biology Test 2		
Biology Test 3		
Biology Test 4		
Biology Test 5		
Biology Test 6		
Chemistry Test 1		
Chemistry Test 2		
Chemistry Test 3		
Chemistry Test 4		
Chemistry Test 5		
Chemistry Test 6		
Physics Test 1		
Physics Test 2		
Physics Test 3		
Physics Test 4		
Physics Test 5		
Physics Test 6		
Mixed Science Test 1		
Mixed Science Test 2		
Mixed Science Test 3		
Mixed Science Test 4		
Mixed Science Test 5		
Mixed Science Test 6		